SWEET SIXTEEN

THOUGHTS TURNED INTO POETRY

ANANYA KARN

I dedicate this book to my parents

for always believing in me and supporting me.

Without you both, I'd have been nothing.

Contents

Contents

Ananya Karn

Ananya Karn is a 16-year-old writer who was born and brought up in Basti, Uttar Pradesh. She originally belongs to Darbhanga, Bihar. She says, "I was an introvert in my childhood and what I can recall now is that I used to scribble in the back pages of my notebook as a 4th grader. Maybe, that's how poetry found me." She became a published author at the age of thirteen. At present, she is a three-time national-level award-winning poet and a co-author of more than 12 books. She writes across various themes and genres without restricting her imagination. To her, "Writing is Healing" and she looks forward to embracing this poetic journey lifelong.

Preface

I've been writing for so long but it was in 2020 that the thought of publishing a book struck me. "Sweet Sixteen" is more than a book to me because it contains me in bits and pieces. It's a collection of poems based on several themes revolving around "teenhood". Indeed as you'd have read on the back of the book cover, it's a roller coaster of emotions.

It is a peek into a sixteen-year-old's head. If you're a teenager, you'll be able to connect deeply with every line. If you're not, reading this might refresh your teenhood memories. I've written this with my whole heart and I hope it would stand up to your expectations.

Hope you'll enjoy reading this.

Acknowledgements

First and foremost, I thank the Almighty God without whose blessings this couldn't have come true.

Next, I would like to thank my parents for always having my back. You both are the lights of my life and I'm nothing without you.

Dear Preeti Di and Priyanka Di,

Thank you for celebrating even my tiniest achievements. Your appreciation keeps me motivated to achieve more.

Dear Sushobhan,

Your presence fills every day with laughter no matter how bad the day would have been. You will always be my partner in crime. Thank you for being the best brother I could have asked for. You make my life complete.

At last, I thank my Yourquote family and friends who always wish the best for me.

I hope I would've been able to live up to all of your's expectations.

- Ananya Karn

"SWEET SIXTEEN" THOUGHTS TURNED INTO POETRY

1. HEALING

pulling a sheet

grabbing an ink pen

scribbling words

dries the ink

days pass;

I read -

scribbled emotions,

dried tears,

healed pain.

2. TAMED

often do I skip rope
in the good name of hope
not for fitness or fun
just to let the beauty business run.

stacked have I creams
and those expensive jeans
to please the judging eyes
whom even God doesn't seem nice.

deep inside I know well
these are making a messy hell
I understand the measures
cannot be true treasures.

six inches high heels,
sacrificing delicious meals,
that's how the world deals
little do they have an idea of how it feels.

'lovely face and long hair
slim waist and skin fair'
will always make you rock
or never will a groom knock.

'tall with a muscular frame
handsome in the hall of fame'
makes you outshine every name
else you're indeed lame.

"brand tags show your wealth;
dollars would buy you love and health
to hide scars which are dark
put on a beautiful mask."

"never dream of peace
or you will fall on your knees
stay greedy if you wish for pride
these are worldly rules to abide".

they shape my choices and me
fail do they in hiding glee
'having sad stories to tell
afraid I am to spell'.

caged I am to impress
with no right to express
in the end, I do find
trapped in a cobweb of minds.

handcuffs surround my hand,
I fight and I defend,
in the race of attaining attention
for impression, perfection, affection:

perishing in the loneliness flame:
I ask myself in a loop - "aren't we tamed?"

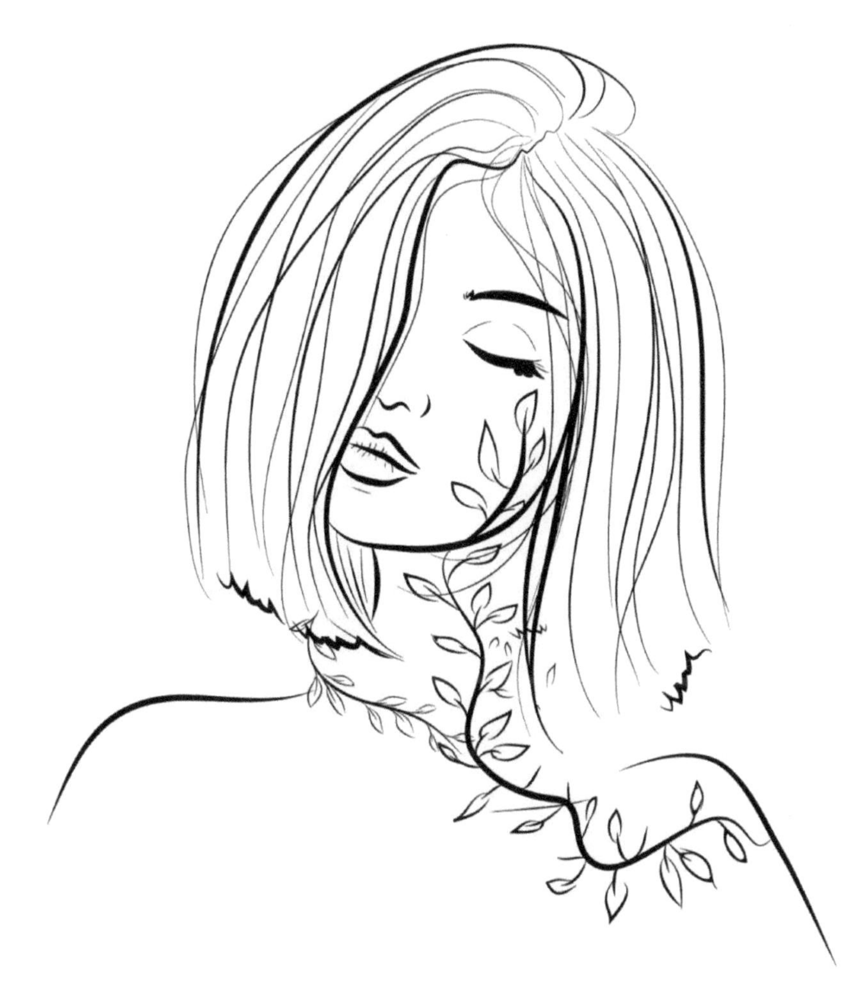

3. GLOOM & BLOOM

Wishing for the bloom
On an eve gloom
Keeping inside the tears
And the fake smile that she wears
Life is like ripped jeans
Harvesting the rotten beans
Ache which was tinkling
Over the eyes which were gladly winking
No-one ever understood
The truth behind eyes in her teenhood
'How cruel the world is!' she used to think
Then tackling the problems she used to blink
The cruelty of the world made her struggle
And her people kept her puzzled
Never did she understand how the person she chattered
Left her with a heart shattered.

4. ARGUMENTS

Screams and noises surrounding
from home to streets to markets
to the office and even
to the miles away at boundaries

I see - I hear
I observe and think
Even not being the odd one out
I beg not to shout

the debate on news channels
the topic being Pakistan or politics
all heated - we watch
forgetting the single root we belong

the cold war between
the elder sons of the family
for property and purse
which proves to be a curse

The men in their forties
at the chai shop with a cup
get into arguments over
the elections and policies

I often see young men
ready to hurt and shed blood
all rebellious not bound to a single rule
as anger is the only tool

the woman in her eighties is a burden
her grown up son argues
the seven vows is a death loop
the violence proves
the silly issues prevail
between the friendships
arguments occur
they mutually continue to suffer

the creator is betrayed
when the religious heat stroke
gets in and destroys the glory

In the end
It's neither me nor you
to be blamed
it's us to be ashamed.

5. WALKING THROUGH GRAVES

Searching the cupboard
upside down for a clothing
I found an album all white
stuffed with memories soothing

The very first picture in the album
was the very first treasure of mine
papa tightly held me in his arms
an hour old me saw him for the first time

Mumma says four year old me
was a fan of sarees
rolling around a pink dupatta
an expert in destroying jewellery

other than girly pictures of mine
I have one all rowdy
with cars and bikes surrounding
it shows my level of being moody

I do remember mum's melodious lullabies
'Little Baby...' she sang

and hatred for schooling made
tears flow my cheeks when the school bell rang

stubborn was me already
motivation was out of the scene
inspiration was never a need
to fulfill my dream

heroes were we in the movie of life
when existed slate chalks, games, and rhymes
snowhite and spiderman ruled our lives
and worldly affairs were only limes

we were perfect in our ways
neither compliments nor comments had place
when self-love had its rays
and publicity was not a case

fights were forgotten
as ego was an unknown crime
justice always remained rotten
when unity was meant to be prime

beautiful years were those
when laughter didn't drain
neither were swords nor were clashes
pure was heart - patient was brain

when ice-pice and kho-kho were played

tactics were never a part of the game
real were joy, pain, and friends
all say childhood was its name

those golden days have vanished
which amazed me in spring and rain
neither did I give nor did anyone take
how did it turn into a 'past' - no-one can explain

'Past never returns'
so won't those golden days
what I am left with at last
are memories, thoughts, pictures that stay

buried in albums
synonym of grave
which makes me live my childhood
little after little, again and again

6. SPEED BREAKERS

so much in my head
even when I am in my bed
clarity is now just a word
as my monkey mind is flying like a bird

academics, passion, aims, and ambitions
future goals like goa vacations
all running in a marathon
not a bit of idea what's right or wrong

they say to be focused and productive
don't they know thoughts are addictive?
it's easy to say not easy to do
dilemma is what I am into

it's not letting me sleep
Oh please! I don't weep
it's not a DDLJ story
neither a tensed theory

it's just that I want to stop
but the fear is about getting flop
will I achieve what I want?

will I have something to flaunt?

would I be with whom I dream?
or remain a story without a theme?
Now please don't teach me to be in the present
from the great philosopher's lesson

I know it - I respect it
It's all correct - it's all right
but this can't offer me a sudden peace
which now seems away from my reach

Stay honest! we all get in such situations
drowning in the river of emotions
I have faced this even before
a moment which I never adore

but it's okay it's not necessary
for a poem to always rhyme
So are days - some high;
some low.

I am a human ;
not a river that would always flow
It's okay if for a day productivity is what I lack
It doesn't mean I am out of track

it's fine to have a break
it never means there is nothing I would make

as far as I know, it's not getting late
null and void would not be my fate

Let me get patient - let me get calm
I know, I cannot be away for long
from the thing which would make me
shine as a charm.

7. MIDNIGHT

The moon among tiny stars
shines all bright
I turn in bed right
and left at midnight

thoughts clutter up
one by one with pride
I get up and sit lonely
in on or off light

thoughts like passengers
pull my sleep aside
start conversations
occupy seats to reside

they introduce themselves
present, future, and past
where the lead role is played
by me in the cast

They discuss with me -
'arguments' - I have been a part
question me - why does the success arrow
seems so far from the dart?

They remind me-
the list of taunts
I have listened to
and things I have taunt

I listen to tick-tock in rhythm
suddenly my ears rise
insects, police, ambulance, trains
whose sounds do surprise

failures and embarrassments
surround my mind
sights flash of people
who weren't ever kind

feelings dipped in ink
I write -
keep them safe and locked
or crush and throw to hide

strong plans I think of
to strive and bounce back
and to fulfill
whatever I lack

I wonder if I am
a person immersed in thoughts
or an insomniac

a disease I have been caught

I think of even
memories which delight
family, love, and friends
people who always guide

I play songs
whose lyrics attach
and paint pictures in the head
of events that match

alarm breaks my voyage
as the ship of thoughts wreck
journey to life begins
when I pick to-do lists to check.

8. VIRTUAL REALITY

shown is the good side
bad is what we hide
appearing to be wise
to get six on the dice

'compliments' - we dream
lowering is our self-esteem
wrong comments don't stay
that's what we pray

memorizing catchy captions
to be the center of attraction
it's all fake - we know
still, we need to bow

empathy continues to low
restricting us to grow
different is real and reel
but this remains conceal

virtues and values they steal
giving wounds that won't heal
authenticity is a joke here
each friend is not dear

opinions are a nightmare
generosity exists nowhere
clicking likes for faces
we are in unknown races

most of us behind the shimmer
failing to look at the mirror
glancing at others' perfect lives
post thoughts serve as knives

toxicity is indeed close
as thorns surround the rose
sorrows are hidden
reality is forbidden

often it appears as a legalized crime
with no punishments in time
long and short conversations
at familiar and strange stations

'brings us closer to everyone
but losing identity feels like no one.'

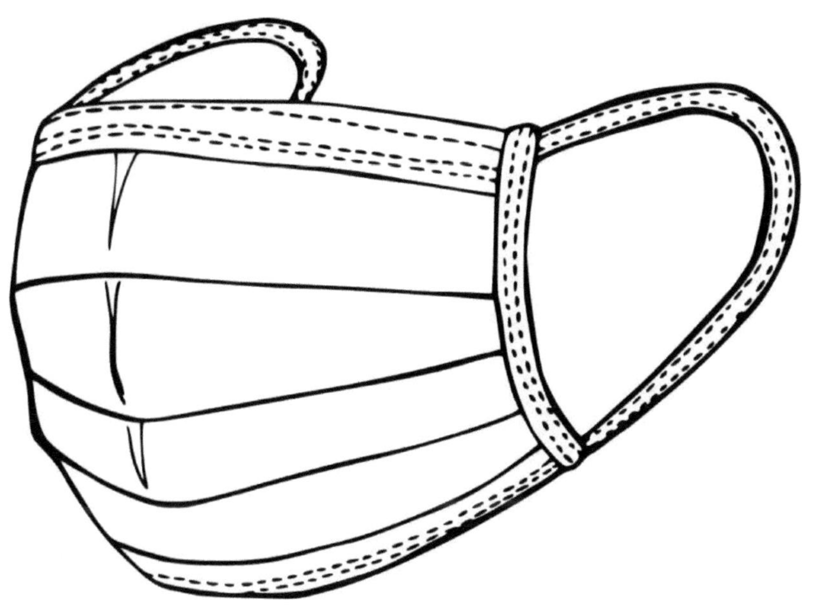

9. UNCERTAINTY - COVID 19

from shattering hearts
to losing dreams
listening are the walls
the unheard screams

becoming orphans
to turning widows
white cloth over bodies
leaves stains as shadows

unfulfilled wishes
unfinished roles
bleeding are eyes
nothing is in control

incomplete love and life
how will they console
the people behind
and the leaving soul?

crowded are hospitals
weeping are the beds

witnessing pathetic destruction
and the depressing dead

caged in homes
caged are giggles
struggling are we
to solve the melancholic riddle

thought had we once
all is in our hand
proved is our worth
a virus we can't withstand

praying are all to end
this deadly disaster
and wishing are we
for God to respond faster

lightening lamps of hope
are the white coats
savior of lives
are these stethoscopes

deaths are being counted
isn't this the darkest phase?
breaths are doubted
a reality we can't erase.

10. PHOENIX

I won't agree
to assumptions about me
I will disagree
to what's wrong to me

this is my life
I will hold it tight
ain't afraid of the knife
I am ready to fight

neither on the 9th cloud
lacks everything proud
nor even in a crowd
just a phoenix on ground

not a matter of luck
just a bird who's stuck
ready to squeeze its chest
to handmade its nest

in a marathon to run
a dreamer in a slum
last hope in the gun
who's dumb to numb

'Bark' if you bark
to make things dark
in return, I won't hate
but create my fate

to reach a certain height
my ashes will unite
to make wings flap
make 'Barks' clap

I haven't loose
just fallen on the track
fastening lace of shoes
I'd bounce back

wait and watch
wars would be won
crowns I'd catch
'Mine' will thrones turn

games would narrate
story of checkmate
"Pawn who's never bend
turns 'Queen' at gate's end"

11. WOMEN & VIOLENCE

Dear women,

you were ditched
and discarded to die
being a newborn angel
as gender can't be switched

you dreamt to fly high
but were found caged
on spreading wings
to touch the mighty sky

somewhere they snatched
books, voice or freedom
somewhere for no good reason
you were found brutally attacked

their hands didn't tremble
to burn or break you with
acid's bottle but you proved
you're strong enough to reassemble

you were burnt in the fire
of their never-ending greed,
balanced with cash and gold
for wedding's senseless need

somewhere you were raised for a life
"Raped" - a headline was observed
unfortunately, you screamed and died
the death you never deserved

by the familiar faces, you loved
you were beaten at your place
still, no one could guess that
domestic violence was a case

somewhere your life and decisions
were predecided by those in power
hence before you could even bloom
you were turned into a withered flower

will this ever end?
every women's heart asks
will things change and society
will ever take off this dirty mask?

let the world know I believe
it sees and listens
but tell it to answer

for these inhuman incidents

If the divinity gives life
it's given to live and not to die
If the divinity has made us human
it's for humanity, a truth you can't deny.

12. THE RAPE STORY

" A night before was foggy
Still, I had dreams all-clear
I knew there would be challenges
Still, I had sworn not to fear

I left the bed the next morning
To unlock the dreams -
all ready to chase
Stepping out of home -
I bid bye to my loving mother
She never knew it was my last phrase

The sun had already set in -
The day was going to end
There were six monsters-
waiting to attempt a crime
Their nails scratched my flesh
I screamed 'maa' for the last time

Every little dream vanished
Everything seemed blurred
I was then declared "Nirbhaya"
After my hands and legs were numbed

The little daughter in me
still wanted to fight
As she wanted to shine bright
My mother's persistent struggle
did bring me justice
But my story still has not ended

As a new "Nirbhaya" rises every other day
Posters, candles, headlines all scream similar pain
But still, nothing is the gain".

13. WOUNDED HEART

in the crowd of millions
to laugh and amuse with
this heart doesn't find solace
it runs to hide or escape
to find a healing space

where it can whisper
all her secrets and stories
without judgements coming her way
where there is peace
and she won't feel torn away

where won't exist dreadful past
where days and nights
won't be a synonym for distress
where she will be set free
and will have the right to express

where humour will exist
where it will learn again
to smile and cackle
where will exist, selfless love,
and won't exist a single battle

this little heart dreams
and prays every night
of such a beautiful castle
where this heart can reside
without a single hassle

this heart is ready to hustle
but not in a world
where the action is a silent attacker
where words can be fatal or
people can make people shatter.

14. TALE OF LOVE

Krishna,

when staring at the moon
became gazing at you
you became constant
from nights to noon.

potion of life,
flew into Radha.

Krishna,

when you became dignity,
her prayers, and her deity.
when you silently turned into
her destination and destiny.

potion of life,
flew into Radha.

Krishna,

when she secretly blushed
with her eyes at your feet

when tootling of your flute
made her secretly rush

potion of life,
flew into Radha.

Krishna,

when with your presence
simple turned special
when she passed every test -
from perseverance to patience.

potion of life,
flew into Radha.

Krishna,

love is all about giving
selflessly without expecting
it's about fighting all odds
and living for loving.

hence,

potion of life,
flew into Radha.

15. EAGLE

Be free like the bird flying in the sky
Be free from all the worries;
With just one thought in mind;
Thought to achieve the goal of being shined.
Be that eagle who flies alone
Instead of the birds who hate to be left lone;
Have that quality of eagle who never surrenders to its prey;
And can be alone whether it's night or day.
Be the eagle instead of the lazy sloth;
Free, alone, fearless, and full of faith.

Printed by Libri Plureos GmbH in Hamburg,
Germany